KU-757-513

1 A Funny Little Face

Carrie and Pete had never been to Cornwall before. But as soon as they saw the beach, they knew this was going to be a great summer holiday.

Mum and Dad had rented a cottage in the village for their stay. The cottage was halfway up a hill and very old, with little windows that opened outwards, and a steep, staircase. The upstairs rooms had sloping ceilings, and the walls were panelled with light-coloured wood, so that it felt like being on board a ship. And from upstairs you could almost see the beach. Certainly you could hear the sea; a kind of steady hiss and roar as the big breakers rolled in. They had only just arrived, so there had been no time to explore yet, but they had driven past the beach on the way to the cottage, and it looked wonderful, with cliffs and rock pools and a huge stretch of golden sand.

The only thing they weren't going to enjoy was their little brother, Tim. To put it mildly, Tim was a pest. He was always following them around, always wanting to do whatever they were doing. And he usually managed to spoil it. Worse still, there were only three bedrooms at the holiday cottage, so Pete and Tim had to share.

"Oh, no!" Pete groaned when he found out. "Have I *got* to have him with me?"

"Yes, you have," Mum said firmly. "And while we're here, I want you both to look after him and play with him, so I can have some time to relax!"

Carrie and Pete were stuck with it. Next morning though, when they all went to the beach, Tim didn't want to play with his brother and sister. So Carrie and Pete left him happily making a sandcastle, while they went off to explore.

Pebbleboy

By Louise Cooper
illustrated by Mark Williams

Contents

PEARSON
Longman

The tide was out, and they walked round the headland, where the sand stretched away smooth and golden for what looked like miles. To their delight there were several enormous caves, with rock pools at their fringes. Pete went into the first cave and started making weird noises to hear the echoes. But Carrie was more interested in something else.

"Look at the shape of the cliff beside the next cave along," she said, when Pete came out. "It looks just like a face."

It did: a craggy, frowning face, with a huge, hooked nose.

"Weird," said Pete. "Let's go and look in the cave." He grinned. "We might find the rest of the person in there!"

The sunlight faded to gloom as they ventured in. This cave was deeper than the first one, and right at the back was a huge, still pool.

"Can't go any further," Pete said, looking at the dark green water. "I reckon that pool's nearly two metres deep."

Carrie was examining the rock face. "There's an amazing pebble here," she said. "It's another face – like a whole head, in fact."

Pete joined her. "Oh, yes, I see what you mean. It's stuck in that crack. Let me see if I can get it out."

At first the pebble wouldn't move, but Carrie found a piece of driftwood, and between them they levered the stone free. It dropped with a soft thud to the sand – and as it fell, a strange sound, like a deep, eerie groan, echoed through the cave and made them jump violently.

"What was *that*?" Carrie asked as the sound died away.

"I don't know." Pete glanced up uneasily. "You don't think the roof's going to collapse, do you?"

She shivered. "I'm not going to wait here and find out!"

She snatched up the pebble and ran from the cave with Pete at her heels. Outside, they looked back, half expecting to see tonnes of rock collapsing behind them. Nothing happened, and after a few moments they relaxed, feeling a bit silly.

"It must have been an echo from somewhere," said Pete. "A wave maybe, breaking against the cliffs further along."

"Yeah. Anyway, I got the stone. Let's have a proper look at it."

The pebble was quite large and very smooth, and it was shaped just like a funny little human head. It even had markings on it suggesting eyes and a wide, grinning mouth.

"It's quite creepy," Carrie said. "Now I've looked at it properly, I don't think I like it."

"Don't like what?" said a voice.

Their hearts missed a beat and they turned, to find Tim standing beside them.

"Don't *do* that!" Carrie said crossly. "Sneaking up on people –"

"I didn't," said Tim, and pointed at the stone. "What've you got there? Show me!"

"A stone." She held it out. She only meant Tim to look, but he snatched it out of her hand.

"*I* want it!" he declared.

"Well, it's ours, so you can't have it." Carrie tried to grab the pebble back. Tim always wanted whatever they had, and usually a fierce "No!" would shut him up. This time, though, it didn't work. Tim *really* wanted the pebble, and started to work up to a tantrum.

"Give it to me!" he yelled. "Or I'll tell Mum you're horrid and smelly and you bash me up!"

Carrie and Pete looked helplessly at each other. Mum always took Tim's side, however unfairly. If he went telling tales, they'd be in trouble.

"Oh, let him have it," said Pete grumpily. "We don't really want it anyway."

Tim smirked. "It's mine now!" he said. Then, as if he had just remembered, he added, "Mum says it's nearly time for our picnic. We've got pasties."

Tim carried 'his' stone very carefully as they all walked back to where Mum and Dad were sitting. As soon as the picnic lunch was finished, he started to gather more stones. When he had a good armful, he went a little way off, plonked himself down on the sand and started to heap them up.

"What's he doing?" Carrie was curious.

Pete shrugged. "Who cares? Just so long as he keeps out of our way. Come on – let's go in the sea!"

Under the watchful eyes of the lifeguards Carrie and Pete spent a terrific afternoon splashing

and jumping around in the waves. When they finally came out, Tim was still exactly where they had left him. So was his pile of stones. But they weren't just a pile of stones any more.

Tim had made a pebble figure on the sand – and Carrie and Pete had to admit that he'd done it really well. Small stones were laid out to form thick little legs, bigger stones made up the body, with two long ones for stumpy arms. And at the top was the pebble Carrie and Pete had found. It really did look uncannily like a strange little person there.

"He's called Pebbleboy," Tim told them proudly. "He's my friend."

Mum and Dad came to look and admire, and Tim basked in praise. But when it was time to pack up and go back to the cottage, his mood changed.

"I'm not leaving Pebbleboy!" he wailed.

"He's my best ever friend, and I want to stay here with him!"

"Don't be so silly," said Mum. "You can't stay here all night."

"Or the tide'll come in and drown you," Pete added with relish.

Mum gave Pete a warning look. "Come on, Tim," she coaxed. "We're having fish and chips tonight. They're your favourites."

"Don't want fish and chips!" Tim bawled. "Want to stay with Pebbleboy!"

He kicked up a fuss, shouting and crying and stamping his feet, until even Mum had had enough. "Right!" she snapped. "No more nonsense – you're coming with us, *now!*"

She and Dad both grabbed one of Tim's hands and marched him off the beach. Carrie and Pete followed, listening to Tim's roars of protest. As they reached the road,

Carrie looked back. They were the last people to leave, and the beach was deserted – but for the funny little figure of Pebbleboy. There he was, facing out to sea, as if he was defying the incoming tide. Carrie smiled to herself. *Some chance*, she thought. The tide was creeping up quickly. In another hour it would reach Pebbleboy and wash him away. Pity, really. Tim had worked hard. Oh, well. He'd probably forget all about it by tomorrow.

2 Come to the Sea ...

Tim didn't forget about Pebbleboy. He sulked for half the evening, refusing to speak to anyone. But just before his bedtime, he suddenly brightened up.

"I know a song," he announced.

"Yeah?" Carrie was sorting through some shells she had collected and wasn't paying attention.

"Yeah," said Tim. "Listen: *Come to the seeea, come with meee, I am freeee!*"

It wasn't really a song at all – more of a drone, without much of a tune.

"That's gross," said Pete. "It sounds like the sort of thing people sing at funerals."

"Isn't!" said Tim. "It's *great*. It's mine and Pebbleboy's song, and I'll sing it as much as I want!"

Which he did, over and over again, and no one could make him stop. He sang it as Mum took him up to bed, he sang it in the bathroom, he

sang it as she tucked him in and said goodnight.
You could hear him from downstairs. Pete pulled
a face. "If I have to listen to that all night, I'll go
nuts," he said.

"He'll get tired of it soon," said Dad. Then he
pulled a face, too. "I hope!"

Tim did stop singing, eventually, and everyone
managed to get a night's sleep. Next morning,
though, he was still talking about Pebbleboy.

"There's going to be trouble when he finds
out Pebbleboy isn't there any more," Carrie
whispered to Pete as they all walked to the beach.
"He'll throw the biggest wobbler ever."

"Well, let's make sure
we're somewhere else
when it happens,"
Pete whispered
back. "If he ..."
He stopped,
staring.

"What?" said
Carrie. Then she,
too, saw what he
was looking at.
"I don't believe it!"

Pebbleboy was
still there on the

sand, exactly where Tim had built him. The tide must have covered him completely, the waves had washed over and over him, and he had survived.

"It's incredible!" said Pete. "Unless Tim superglued him together ..."

"Of course he didn't! It's just one of those freak things that happens sometimes." Carrie grinned. "Let's be grateful. It'll keep Tim off our backs!"

Tim spent the whole day with Pebbleboy. He sat beside him, talked to him, brought seaweed and shells to show him. He wasn't interested in whatever Carrie and Pete did; he had games of his own. Games with Pebbleboy. And to everyone's surprise, when it was time to go, he didn't make a fuss.

"S'all right," he said. "I'll see Pebbleboy again tomorrow. Or if he wants, he can come round our house."

Carrie and Pete raised eyebrows but said nothing. It seemed safer.

* * * * *

Tim behaved himself all evening and went to bed as good as gold. He didn't even stir when Pete came in later, and Pete fell happily, tiredly asleep.

Not for long, though. Soon after midnight, something woke him. He opened his eyes, blinking … then heard a noise. A droning noise.

"*Come to the sea, come with me, I am free …*"

That song again! Furious, Pete sat up and switched the bedside lamp on. He opened his mouth to tell Tim to shut up or else – then stopped as he saw that the other bed was empty.

The droning song was coming from downstairs.

"Oh, *great!*" Pete scrambled out of bed and headed for the door. No need to wake Mum and Dad, he thought; he'd deal with the horrible little brat himself.

Though maybe he could use some help from Carrie …

He knocked softly on Carrie's door. "Carrie? You awake?"

"Yeah," came her voice from inside. "Can't you make Tim shut up?"

"I would, if I knew where he was!" Opening the door, Pete told his sister what had happened, and together they headed along the landing.

The front door had a blue glass panel, and moonlight was shining through it into the little hall. So as they reached the top of the steep, narrow stairs, they saw Tim at once. He was at the door, trying to reach the bolt at the top to undo it.

Carrie ran down the stairs and grabbed him. "Tim! What do you think you're doing?"

Tim glared at her. "Want to open the door," he said.

"Well, you can't!"

"Want to! For Pebbleboy."

"*Pebbleboy?*" Carrie began to lose her temper. "Don't be so stupid! Pebbleboy's on the beach – he's not real, he can't walk!"

"Yes, he can! If he wants to!"

There was no point in arguing. "Look," said Carrie fiercely, "you are going back to bed right this minute, or I'm going to fetch Mum! Do you want me to do that?"

Tim pouted. "No-o ..."

"Then get upstairs, *now!*"

To their relief, Tim did as he was told. They tucked him back into his bed, said goodnight, and Carrie returned to her own room. Hand on the door handle, she paused suddenly as she thought she heard something. Just a small sound, from the direction of the stairs. What was it?

Carrie turned slowly and peered into the darkness along the landing. She couldn't see anything. But she could still hear it. Like something moving.

And as it moved, it *clicked* ...

Her heart started to thump a little. Not that she was spooked – of course not. There had to be an explanation. There always was. *Come on Carrie; take a look. Just a quick one.*

She tiptoed back to the top of the staircase. Moonlight still shone into the hall. There was nothing there. Nothing at all. And the noise had stopped now. *I must have imagined it,* she told herself.

She turned to go back to her room. Then just for a moment, in the moonlit hall, a small shadow seemed to move ...

Carrie jumped, blinked and looked again.

There wasn't a shadow. She had been right first time: there was nothing there at all.

Feeling foolish, but relieved, Carrie went back to bed.

3 A Voice in the Night

When they all arrived at the beach the next morning, to their astonishment Pebbleboy was still there. Only Tim didn't seem surprised. Again, he spent all day with the little stone figure. But when they packed up to leave, he suddenly threw a tantrum.

Tim wanted to take Pebbleboy home. Carrie and Pete argued, and Mum tried to reason with him, saying he could see Pebbleboy again tomorrow. It didn't make a scrap of difference: Tim yelled and screamed, and kicked Pete, and threw sand at everyone. At last even Mum couldn't stand any more and gave in. So Tim took Pebbleboy apart, very carefully, and put all the stones in his red beach bucket. The full bucket was too heavy for him to carry, so Dad had to do it. Dad grumbled all the way back to the cottage. But Tim was happy.

There was another fuss when they got back,
though, because Tim wanted to reassemble
Pebbleboy in the bedroom he shared with Pete.
Pete flatly refused. "I don't want that thing staring
at me all night," he pleaded. "It gives me the
creeps!"

Carrie backed Pete up. Neither of them wanted
to admit it, but they both felt that there was
something a bit spooky about Pebbleboy. The
stone Tim had used to make his head looked more
like a face than ever. A face with mean little eyes.
And the grin on the mouth wasn't a pleasant grin
at all.

Perhaps Mum and Dad felt the same
way, for Pebbleboy stayed
downstairs. Tim put him
back together on the
table in the sitting room,
and there he stayed,
staring at them
all while they
watched TV.
Carrie and
Pete tried
not to look
at him
too often.

21

They just hoped that Tim would get bored and lose interest in him before too long.

Sun and sea air are tiring. So Carrie was surprised, and a little annoyed, when she woke up in the middle of the night. There was no reason for her to be awake. Tim wasn't singing his song next door, and there was no sound from outside. Even the sea was quiet. But Carrie could tell that she wasn't going to get back to sleep.

Then she began to have a strange urge to look out of the window. The feeling crept up slowly, and started to nag at her.

Nag, nag, nag …

Go away, she told it silently.

Nag, nag, nag … It wouldn't leave her alone. *All right, then,* she thought. *I'll go and look. And then perhaps I can forget it and have some peace!*

She padded across the floor and pulled the curtain back. The moon was high in the sky, casting cool, silvery light across the village. In the distance Carrie could make out the dark humps of the cliffs. She could hear the sea now. At least, she thought it must be the sea. Though it didn't sound quite right, somehow. The sea hissed. This was more of a *rumbling*.

Suddenly the rumbling grew louder. An aircraft? Or even thunder?

Curious, Carrie opened the window to hear better.

And the rumbling sound changed into a deep voice, weirdly distorted and echoey, that boomed out of the night.

LITTLE BOY ... GIVE ME MY LITTLE BOY ...

Where the cliffs had been a moment ago, a huge, dark shape was rising. It loomed towards Carrie's window, blotting out the moon and the stars. Carrie's eyes bulged; she screamed – and woke up, to find herself still in bed, with the booming voice gone.

Carrie gasped with shock. It had been a dream; only a dream. But for a few moments it had seemed so *real*.

She sat up in bed and fumbled for the switch of her bedside lamp. Then, as she flicked the light on, she heard singing.

"Come to the sea, come with me, I am free ..."

Tim was droning that awful song again. It set Carrie's teeth on edge – no wonder she had had a nightmare, with that going on in the next room! Well, she wasn't going to put up with it. She had had all she was prepared to take from Tim. This time, she was going to sort the little pest out once and for all.

She reached the door in three strides, jerked it open – and came face to face with Pete on the landing.

"Hi," she said, her voice full of sympathy. "What shall we do – kill him now, or save him for later?"

"Who?" said Pete. Carrie saw that his face was pale and she frowned, puzzled.

"Tim, of course."

Pete said, "Tim's fast asleep. Whoever's singing that song, it isn't him."

Carrie's eyes widened. "What?"

"He's asleep," Pete repeated. "In his bed."

She gulped. "Then who ..."

"I don't know." Pete let out a deep breath. "I thought I was imagining things. But if you can hear it, too ..."

Who, or what, is singing it? The drone was still going on, and a chill went through Carrie as she suddenly realised that the voice didn't actually sound like Tim's.

"Sh-should we wake Mum and Dad?" she whispered.

"No-o …" Pete said, though he didn't seem too certain. "I think we ought to take a look downstairs first. I've got a torch."

It took all their courage to go quietly along the landing and start down the staircase. Halfway down, Carrie stopped and sniffed the air.

"Can you smell anything?" she whispered.

Pete wrinkled his nose. "Now you mention it – yes. Something sort of – salty. Tangy."

Carrie nodded. The smell was very strong, and she

thought she recognised it. "Seaweed," she said.

"That's it! And look at the next stair. It's wet!"

She looked, and saw the gleam on the bare wood. There were puddles of water, too, on the next step and the next; in fact, all the way down to the hall.

"Come on," said Pete with grim determination. "Let's find out what's going on."

They continued down. Then, just as they reached the hall, the singing stopped.

"It was coming from the sitting room, I'm sure of it," said Carrie.

The sitting room door was shut. They crept up to it, and slowly Pete turned the handle. The door swung back and he shone the torch inside.

There was no one in the room. Everything was exactly as it had been when they went to bed. Except ...

Carrie pointed to the table. "Pebbleboy's gone!"

He had. The tray that Mum had made Tim put him on (so the table wouldn't be marked) was still there, but Pebbleboy was no longer on it.

Then, from behind them, came a soft, shuffling sound. The hairs on Carrie's neck rose. Pete's heart started to pound. They looked at each other, breathless, too scared to turn round ...

4 Where's Pebbleboy?

"Boo!" said Tim.

He was standing behind them, barefoot and in his Batman pyjamas.

"*Ohhh!*" Carrie let out her breath, relieved and angry at the same time. "If you do that to me again ..."

Tim grinned. "Scared you!"

"No, you didn't!" She pointed to the table. "What have you been up to? Where's Pebbleboy?"

Tim's grin became secretive, and he replied, "He's runned away."

"What?"

"His Mummy's cross with him, and he runned away so she won't catch him."

"His Mummy?" Pete's voice was just a tiny bit uneasy. "What do you mean, Tim?"

"His Mummy's big," said Tim. "Ever so big. *This* big!" He stood on tiptoe, spreading his arms as wide as he could. Then, as if he was telling a secret, he added, "She says Pebbleboy's naughty to run away. But he doesn't care!"

With a shiver Carrie recalled her dream. That huge, rumbling voice, and the words it had said: *GIVE ME MY LITTLE BOY* ... And she remembered the cave where she and Pete found the head-shaped stone. And the groaning noise that had frightened them both when they had got it free ...

Pete didn't know about the dream, and he glared at Tim. "He's talking rubbish, as usual," he said to Carrie. "Come on, Tim. You've hidden Pebbleboy somewhere, haven't you?"

"Haven't. He runned away, like I said."

"He didn't run away, because he can't. Tell us where he is!"

Tim just shook his head, and no matter how hard Pete tried, he wouldn't own up to hiding Pebbleboy. He stuck firmly to his "runned away" story, and at last Pete gave up. "Come on,"

he said to Carrie. "We'd better take him back to bed, before Mum wakes up."

Tim didn't argue as they led him upstairs and put him in bed. But as Carrie and Pete tucked him in, he smiled slyly at them.

"I'm not scared of Pebbleboy's Mummy," he said. "I know where he is. He told me. I'm going to play with him, 'cos he's my *friend*." And he started to sing: "*Come to the sea, come with me, I am free …*"

"Pete," Carrie said under her breath, "come back to my room for a minute. I want to tell you something."

They left Tim still singing, and in Carrie's room she described her dream to Pete.

"Urgh." Pete pulled a face. "That's spooky!" He paused. "There's something seriously weird about this whole Pebbleboy thing, isn't there?"

"Too right," Carrie agreed. "The way Tim keeps on about him as if he's alive – it's giving me the creeps. And after some of the things that have happened, well … I'm starting to wonder if Tim's right."

"Look" said Pete, "let's be sensible. Pebbleboy *isn't* alive, because that sort of thing can't possibly happen. Tim's hidden him and won't tell us where, that's all. It's just a stupid game he's playing."

"Well, I don't like it!"

"Neither do I. In fact, I think it's about time we stopped it, and I think I know how. In the morning, we'll find those stones. They've got to be in the house somewhere, and there aren't many places Tim can reach. When we've got them, we'll take them to the beach and throw them in the sea, as far out as we can."

"Yes," said Carrie with relief, starting to feel better. "That's a great idea."

"Right. We agree, then. Now we'd better try and get some sleep."

* * * * *

Carrie fell asleep again quite quickly – but the
nightmare came back. Again she found herself
standing at the window, and again a huge, deep
and distorted voice was calling, *"GIVE ME MY
LITTLE BOY ..."*

For some reason, however, the voice didn't
frighten Carrie in the way it had done before.
Instead, she felt almost
sorry for it, and she
opened the window to
call back.

"All right!" she
shouted in her dream.
"You can *have* him!
But first I've got to
find out where he is!"

Instantly, the
rumbling voice stopped.
She had the strange
feeling that something
she couldn't see was
listening, waiting for
her to speak again.

"Look," she called nervously,
"I can't promise anything. But I'll try. I
really will!"

The voice did not answer. But from the

direction of the beach, a vast shadow, big as a cliff, started to rise against the night sky and loom towards her …

Carrie woke up with a jolt. There was no voice, no shadow. The dream had gone, and the house was dark and quiet.

Too quiet, in fact. Carrie couldn't explain why, but she had a feeling that something was wrong, and the longer she lay there thinking about it, the stronger the feeling became. Maybe, she thought, she would look in to Pete and Tim's room. Just quickly. Just to make sure everything was all right.

She opened the boys' door very quietly. Her eyes were used to the dark, and she could see that Pete was asleep. Then she looked at the other bed.

It was empty.

5 The Incoming Tide

"Pete – Pete, wake up!"

Pete grumbled and growled at being shaken roughly awake. And when he found out why Carrie had woken him, he was furious.

"This time I really will *murder* him!" he snarled.

"Join the queue!" said Carrie. "Come on. We'd better go and find him again."

The splashes of water were still on the stairs, but the peculiar, seaweedy smell had gone. Pete reached the hall first. He shone the torch –

"Carrie! The front door's open!"

"Oh, God …" She looked at him, horrified, as they both remembered what Tim had said a few hours ago when they took him back to bed.

"He's gone looking for Pebbleboy!" said Pete.

They checked the house to make absolutely sure. But it only took them two minutes to confirm that Tim had gone.

"His bucket's still here, though," Carrie said. "So if he did hide the stones, he hasn't taken them with him."

"He couldn't carry them, anyway," Pete reminded her. "No. He's got some crazy idea that Pebbleboy's gone off somewhere, and he's gone after him."

"The beach, then," said Carrie. "It's the obvious place!"

They exchanged frightened looks as they both thought the same thing. The tide would be coming in …

"Quick," said Pete. "We'd better get some shoes on and find him!"

* * * * *

The first glimmer of dawn was in the sky as Carrie and Pete set off for the beach. As they ran through the empty streets they could hear the sea. It sounded frighteningly close. Carrie thought of

Tim, on his own, too young to really understand how dangerous the tide could be, and she made herself run faster, breathlessly urging Pete to hurry.

When they reached the beach, there was just enough light for them to see that it was deserted.

The incoming tide wasn't past the headland yet, and they raced to the water's edge. The whole scene was grey and dim, and for a few moments they saw nothing. Then Pete cried, "There he is!"

In the distance, a little figure was walking along the sand. He had his back to them, and he was heading towards the very end of the beach, where a huge, frowning headland jutted out with the waves crashing and foaming around it.

He was not alone. Another figure, much smaller and squatter than Tim, was stumping along beside him.

Carrie and Pete looked at each other in disbelief.

"It can't be ..." Carrie whispered.

Pete swallowed. "I know it can't. But ..." He couldn't finish. He couldn't find the words.

Then Carrie forgot Pebbleboy as a new fear hit her. "Pete," she said, her voice shaking. "Look where they're going!"

Tim and whatever was beside him were getting dangerously close to the end of the beach. A few more minutes and they would reach the headland and the surging tide – and Tim didn't seem to care. He just kept steadily walking.

"Run!" Carrie cried. "We've got to get to him, before it's too late!"

They pounded desperately over the sand. The sea's hiss and roar grew louder and louder, but still Tim walked on.

"Tim!" they shouted. *"Tim!"*

Tim looked back and saw them. Then he broke into a run, the little figure shambling beside him.

"He's trying to get away!" Pete gasped. "Come *on*, Carrie!"

Tim did his best to escape, but Carrie and Pete were faster runners. They caught up with him about twenty metres from the end of the beach,

and grabbed him. Tim struggled and wriggled, but they hung on to his arms, and at last he stopped fighting and glared defiantly at them.

"Go away!" he shouted. "I'm going to the sea with Pebbleboy!"

Carrie and Pete had forgotten everything else in their frantic effort to stop Tim. But now Carrie flung a look over her shoulder. Pebbleboy stood on the sand a couple of metres away. He wasn't moving. He wasn't alive. He was nothing more than a little figure made from a pile of stones.

But we saw him moving, Carrie thought. *We did. I know we did.*

Suddenly she had the crazy feeling that Pebbleboy was secretly laughing at them. That horrible face, with the nasty eyes and grinning, mocking mouth … She *hated* him. She wanted to get *rid* of him.

She pounced on the little figure. Tim yelled in protest, but Carrie didn't care. She grabbed at the stones, meaning to take Pebbleboy apart and scatter him all over the sand.

She couldn't do it. It was as if the stones had been glued together, and however hard Carrie tried, she could not move them. Horrified, she started to kick Pebbleboy – but even that was useless; she only hurt her toes.

Then, with a heart-thumping shock, a sound rang out. An eerie groan that changed to a deep, warning rumble … It echoed across the beach, drowning out the noise of the sea. It was the sound that Carrie and Pete had heard and thought was a rock fall. It was the sound that Carrie had heard in her dream.

And it was coming from the cave where they had found the strange stone that made Pebbleboy's head.

6 A Perfectly Ordinary Beach

Carrie and Pete spun round to face the cave – and their hearts nearly stopped beating altogether.

The rocks at the cave mouth had changed. They didn't just *look* like a face now. They *were* a face. Bulging stone eyes stared at them above craggy cheeks. Nostrils flared in the huge, hooked nose. And the rock crevice that formed the mouth was *moving!*

A gust of wind rushed from the cave towards them, and the rumbling became a gigantic voice that dinned in their ears.

"GIVE ME MY LITTLE BOY!"

Carrie and Pete clutched each other. The voice boomed out again.

"BRING HIM TO ME! BRING HIM AND YOUR BROTHER WILL BE SAFE."

Pete looked as if he was about to be sick with terror – but Carrie realised suddenly that there was nothing to be afraid of. She knew what she must do. She must take Pebbleboy back to the cave!

She grabbed at Pebbleboy again. But Pebbleboy wouldn't move. Frantically Carrie pulled and tugged. Then she jumped back with a yelp as a sharp pain shot through her fingers.

"It bit me!"

"Serves you right!" Tim shouted, furious. "You've made Pebbleboy cross! He'll *get* you now!"

To Carrie's horror, Pebbleboy started to move menacingly towards her.

"No ..." She backed away. Pebbleboy followed. "No, stop it! Pete – *do* something!"

Pete made a lunge at Pebbleboy, but he too sprang back with a shout of pain. Nursing his fingers, he ran to Carrie and stood between her and Pebbleboy.

"Go away! Get back!" Pete waved his arms menacingly. Pebbleboy took no notice. He kept coming.

"Pete," Carrie hissed. "Lead him to the cave!"

Pete understood – it was what the voice wanted. They backed towards the cave mouth. Pebbleboy came after them.

Suddenly from the cave came another deep rumble – and Carrie and Pete both screamed as two long spurs of rock erupted out of the sand to either side of them. They and Pebbleboy were enfolded as if by enormous arms, which started to close in.

Pete shouted: *"Run!"*

With another thunderous rumble the rocks came

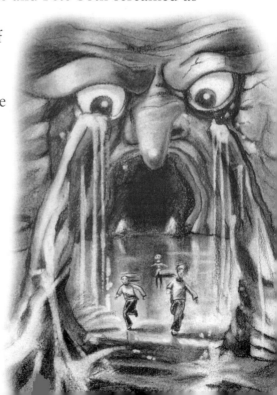

sweeping together. Carrie and Pete pelted for the narrowing gap, and hurled themselves through as the two arms met with a deafening crash, trapping Pebbleboy between them.

Carrie sprawled, winded, on the sand. Pete was beside her. He sat up and gasped, "Look!"

Carrie raised her head and stared. The rock arms were rising into the air. She could see hands, she really could, clasping the struggling Pebbleboy. Then the arms folded inwards, and Pebbleboy was carried into the cave. He vanished into the darkness. From the cave's depths came a great, soft sigh of relief – and for a dizzying moment the world seemed to turn upside down. The sound of the sea faded, came back again …

And Carrie and Pete found themselves on a perfectly ordinary beach, in perfectly ordinary dawn light. The rock arms were gone. The sand was smooth. And the craggy cliff didn't look like a face at all.

For several seconds they were too shocked to do anything. They just stayed where they were, mouths open, eyes goggling. Then, in a quavering whisper, Carrie asked, "Did that really happen?"

Pete gulped. "I don't know," he whispered back. "I think …" But he didn't know what he thought, so the words trailed off into silence.

Suddenly Carrie said, "Tim! Where's Tim?"

They swung round in alarm. Two metres away, Tim lay curled up on the sand.

"He's fast asleep!" Carrie said in wonder.

They tried to wake their little brother, but Tim only mumbled in his sleep and wouldn't stir.

"Looks like we'll have to carry him," said Pete. "Ready? Heave!"

Between them they carried Tim away from the beach and towards the house. They didn't talk on the way, though they both kept looking back at the beach. Nothing was following them. Nothing was there.

Tim still didn't wake as they put him to bed. They stood looking down at him, and Pete asked, "Do you think he'll remember in the morning?"

"Who knows?" said Carrie. She glanced out of the window and thought of her dream. Softly, she whispered, "*Thank you.*"

"What?" said Pete.

"Nothing," said Carrie. She gave the sleeping Tim a kiss, and went back to her room.

* * * * *

In the morning, everything was absolutely normal. Tim was bright and lively and being a pest, but he didn't mention Pebbleboy. He seemed to have forgotten all about him, as though Pebbleboy had never existed.

The whole family went to the beach as usual.

In the morning the tide was too high for Carrie and Pete to reach the cave. But after lunch, when the tide went out, they walked round the headland.

Though the cave looked as ordinary as everything else, they had to steady their nerves before going inside. Nothing spooky happened, and after a couple of minutes they ventured right to the back. There was the deep pool, and nearby was the crack in the rock. Stuck in the crack was a large pebble.

The pebble looked exactly like a funny little human head.

Carrie and Pete met each other's gazes, and Carrie felt a small, chilly shiver go through her.

"This time," she said, "I think we'll leave it alone."

Pete nodded. "Yeah," he agreed. "I think we will."

They walked back out into the sunlight.